Keely Nugent

CHANGE
BRING IT ON!

A simple, workable framework for leading and managing successful business transformation

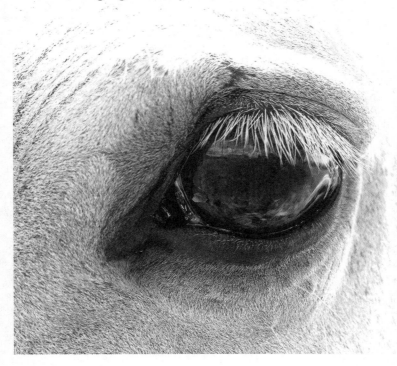

Copyright © Keely Nugent, 2010

The right of Keely Nugent to be identified as the author of this book has been asserted in accordance with the Copyright, Designs and Patents Act 1988.

First published in 2010 by

Infinite Ideas Limited

36 St Giles

Oxford

OX1 3LD

United Kingdom

www.infideas.com

A CIP catalogue record for this book is available from the British Library

ISBN 978-1-906821-51-7

Brand and product names are trademarks or registered trademarks of their respective owners.

Designed and typeset by Cylinder

Illustrations by Victor Lunn-Rockliffe

Printed and bound in Great Britain by Bell and Bain Ltd., Glasgow

CONTENTS

ACKNOWLEDGEMENTS

Being a business consultant not a thespian I never thought I would give an Oscar acceptance speech. This assumption was correct! However I do feel that this is my time, with tears running down my cheeks, to thank most deeply those people without whose help this book would never have been written.

My thanks first and foremost go to Victor Lunn-Rockliffe who not only did all the drawings in the book but from the beginning understood the synergy between horse and business, and has supported me in capturing it for the reader. I do believe that without Victor's guidance, counsel and enthusiasm the book would still have been on my 'must do' list. My thanks also must go to Lucy Thompson who gave me the insight into developing horses that led to the framework that forms the backbone of the book.

However, my thank yous are not finished yet. In the writing of this book I have been extremely lucky to receive emotional and professional support from many excellent business people and friends. From David Russell who had absolute belief in my ability to write a book and whose comment on my first (admittedly very short) draft was 'very good but it's a pamphlet not a book – more work needed!' to Colin Muid (mature wisdom with a hint of magic) and Steve Tibble who were tremendously generous with their business expertise, advice and time, thank you. My thanks also go to John Cameron and Linda Shipley for their support with the 'suggested activities' section at the end of each chapter, which helped turn the book into a really useful business tool and allowed me to write those all important last 9000 words.

I have many more people to thank but fear that by listing names I shall inadvertently omit some. So I shall merely give a big thank you to everyone who has so generously helped me, you know who you are. I am a very lucky person to have had your support.

And last but not least a big thank you to my horses from which there is so much to learn and who continue to be an inspiration to me.

I definitely feel like a thespian now!

Keely

INTRODUCTION

Businesses need to evolve. This is even truer in today's economy. Businesses need to change whether they like it or not in order to survive in today's ever-changing world. Most leaders and managers approach the thought of change with horror. Hardly surprising, when they're being asked to focus on so many areas – sustaining client loyalty, reducing costs, increasing cash, maximising the use of technology, realising the potential of the employee base, etc., etc... The list is endless and daunting. Added to this, a lot of leaders and managers probably have little experience of either leading or managing in a change environment, many having started their careers after the last recession of the early 90s. In the old days – say a year ago – such managers would have brought in consulting firms to effect the change; they would have been one step removed from the action – and the buck. Today, this isn't an option. Today, due to economic necessity, and like it or not, leading and managing business change is being brought firmly in-house.

I've worked in business for the last twenty-five years across a variety of industries, all of which were at different stages of their development. Through some quirk of fate I've always ended up in the middle of some form of change, be it through acquisition, merger, market dynamics, technology or just good old-fashioned change of leadership.

I must be honest. I can't say that my experience of change in the workplace has been a wholly pleasurable one. What I can say is that I have had a very interesting journey which has taught me a lot. However, I remain frustrated and dismayed at the amount of emotional turmoil, business uncertainty and sheer pain that organisations, their leaders and employees go through in the name of change. With around 70% of change initiatives being viewed as failing to deliver (according to a *Harvard Business Review* survey), there must be another way.

My gut feeling from my own experiences and those of colleagues and friends has always been that we go out of our way to make something which could be very simple (not easy, I hasten to add), complex.

We're often satisfied with only a sketchy view of where we want to get to or the steps we need to take to get there, an even sketchier view of the state our organisation is in and no realistic picture of our return on investment. Added to this, we then embark on a plan to achieve the change which is usually some three years or more in duration, and with benefits delivered only at the end of this period. It usually necessitates the running of multiple work streams that operate in silos and very often fail to deliver. And, if one was to be completely negative, detracts from the day-to-day profitable running of the business.

Many times business leaders fail to lead through lack of vision, lack of conviction, lack of skills or just plain fear of failure. Employees buck against change through a lack of an understanding of what's required of them, fear of the unknown or fear of failure and then, unsurprisingly, fail by mere osmosis to acquire and embrace new skills and ways of working. Feels familiar? I'm sure it does...

My own experience of the elements of change had suggested that it was complex. But, as I said, in my gut I didn't believe it. I was sure that it was all a matter of process. If you looked at change simply enough, it would become simple. If you tried to make it complex, it would be complex. I knew that I could make it simple – but how? I set out to find another way and discovered it in the most unlikely of sources.

This book is about the other way. It outlines a very simple but effective way of approaching change and the process of change. It has been used in practice, and has produced world-beating results.

Why you need to read this book

Change, bring it on! shares a very simple but effective way of leading and approaching business change and the process of change. It takes a tried and tested approach used in the preparation of horses for international competition, and mirrors it on to the world of business. It is an approach which is, without a doubt, worth copying – because it consistently produces those world-beating results.

Horses are already being used to support corporate and individual learning. The use of horses isn't surprising as they come with their own personality, behaviours, attitudes and extremely acute senses. They detect fear, anger and any incongruence between actions and emotions. More importantly, horses reflect these disconnections back through their own behaviours.

Leading and developing horses requires vision, focus, intention, energy, empathy and influence – very similar skills to those required in the workplace. It's therefore not surprising that professionals in the competitive world of horses have formulated a foolproof framework for developing or 'bringing on' these complex animals, a methodology that is both harmonious with their nature and delivers quantifiable results every time.

The methodology (as shared with me by former European Three-Day Event Champion, Lucy Thompson) is simple and repeatable. What this book does is very simple too – it provides a tried and tested framework for effecting successful change.

Change, bring it on! follows two interconnecting stories which take the same path. The first is the story of the horse Zircon and his journey of change; the second, the comparable story of a fictionalised company called Zircon Ltd. Both have a new leader, both leaders are committed to helping realise Zircon's potential, both demonstrate the need for the leaders to work together with each element of Zircon and the shared responsibility they have for achieving success.

This is the story of how to lead and establish a winning team; how to vision, plan and manage change; how to overcome the inevitable hiccups which happen along the way and, above all, how to achieve change which always has a beneficial outcome.

This book is for everyone who is planning, leading or experiencing change. It has been designed to make you think in a different way, to help you gain a different perspective, to help you see the wood from the trees and understand the role you need to play. It will help you realise that it can't be achieved alone, that leader and organism (or, should I say, organisation) must be in sync and that successful relationships are two-way relationships, ones requiring commitment and work from both parties, and which are mutually beneficial.

Follow Zircon the horse's story to jolt you out of your usual world, to help you view change through a different lens. Or follow the Zircon Ltd story, and use the pictures accompanying both to help kick-start a new way of thinking, or read each chapter in its entirety to give you a truly compelling case for making change simple. Put what you have learned into practice and use the chapter headings as your framework for organising both your thoughts and actions. Share the book, too; use it to facilitate discussions around your change programme. As it will show, change is something we cannot do alone.

However, if you are one of the lucky few who get it right all the time, perhaps this book isn't for you. Or is it? Open your mind to new possibilities and see!

Who needs to read this book?

You!

Change, bring it on! is for you if you are a leader or manager at any level of an organisation, be it a board member, a department head, a middle manager or a team leader, and will be equally useful for those of you who are running their own show. In fact, I could argue that it should be essential reading for anyone who is planning, leading or managing change in the business environment.

On another level it would also be extremely useful if you are an employee, someone to whom change is effectively 'being done'. It could help you understand the process, what you can expect and the responsibility you personally need to take for the success of any change initiative.

Let me tell you a secret...

When I was seventeen I learned to ride a horse. Not well, but I learned to ride one. Little was I to know that horse riding would become my passion, my driver and inspiration.

Many years later, I was given a mature horse that was extremely naughty, didn't have very good conformation (i.e. she had four legs but not on the most well-proportioned body) or a great love of humans. However, as she was offered to me free of charge and as I was pretty poor at the time, she was my only option and – as she was so horrible and no one really wanted her – I was her only option too.

Gemini wasn't very good at anything. To be honest, she didn't really want to be. But I had a goal for her: I wanted her to find her niche, to be good at just one thing and prove all her detractors wrong. I looked at what I had. Her temperament and conformation weren't any good for either dressage or show jumping but she liked going fast and could go on forever. With this as my foundation I chose to do endurance, which meant covering a specified distance (usually twenty-five miles or over) within a set time. So we had a shared goal – and all we then had to do was put in place a plan to achieve it...

The first part of the plan was to establish myself as leader. The second was to take a phased approach to make us as flexible, strong and fit as possible so we would be agile enough to deal with any terrain or obstacles we might come up against. The third part was to establish a partnership, an interdependent relationship we both took responsibility for, one where we both understood what we needed to deliver. Progress was built on success with lots of praise for even the smallest achievement.

And we did really well at endurance. I didn't realise it at the time, but my blueprint for business change had begun to take shape.

By February 2003 I had purchased a young horse who was stabled at the yard of former Open European Three-Day Event Champion (1995–1997), Lucy Thompson. I hoped, with Lucy's help, to build and develop both my horse and myself so that we could compete and win in our chosen field, but I got much more than I bargained for. I had my eureka moment!

Lucy's yard was a completely new experience for me. I had never previously been exposed to the professional world of horses. I watched Lucy working with her pupils, discussing their goals for their horses and what steps they needed to take to achieve them. Over the time I was there I saw young horses mature, nervous riders grow in confidence, mature horses no longer refuse the water jumps which had troubled them for years (water jumps have monsters in them, you know). I watched many a debrief on what had gone wrong and what had worked well at events. I watched the bad habits of both horse and rider be replaced over time by new, more effective habits. I watched people fall off and get back on again. I watched horses and riders learn to trust one another, depend on one another. I watched success being celebrated. I watched positive progress being made – constantly. I watched a lot.

The child in me liked to think that all this positive progress was happening by luck alone; it meant I wouldn't have to work too hard to make my young horse successful. But the adult in me knew that this couldn't possibly be true, that this success was repeated too often to be down to luck. I could see many elements at play but couldn't see how they fitted together. There just had to be a secret, and Lucy had the key.

Through speaking to and working with Lucy and being coached by her, I gained an insight into how to create world-beating partnerships with horses. Moreover, in tapping into her wealth of experience in preparing top-class horses and riders to compete on the world stage, I was given an insight into a tried and tested method for creating successful change – a way of managing change which has been developed, refined and employed by champion professionals over many decades. But what was uncanny was that the more I learned, the more synergies I could see between creating successful change in horses and creating successful change in businesses.

I worked with Lucy to capture the process and in doing so – and in applying it myself both on a business level and on a personal level when bringing on my horse – I came to understand many things. Among them were what it was like to be a successful leader, and what it felt like to experience a loss of confidence as a leader and to pick myself up and continue leading, and what it felt like to experience success and to go from strength to strength. I also learned to appreciate the sheer power of a successful partnership and came to understand how change was much more likely to succeed if the biggest priorities were focused on first. I also realised the sheer amount of effort it takes to change a less than effective habit into a good habit!

Most importantly, I got to understand how to successfully manage the whole process – how to successfully manage change, how successful partnerships are built and sustained, and how a return on investment can always be guaranteed. It's really very simple. This book will let you into the secret.

But just before I do move on, let me describe a situation which arose while I was writing this. Many business people from both the public and private sector were very kind and reviewed the book and its contents. Many of their comments have been taken on board and the book is what it is today because of their input. However, one person felt that the horse concept was stretched a bit far, but I could confidently tell them it wasn't. The chapters in this book exactly mirror the process as I captured it from Lucy; in the main, the headings too are Lucy's. I have mirrored the business situation directly on to the horse situation. Perhaps the biggest difference between the two is that people in the professional horse world have created a framework for change within the horse, one which they stick to and improve incrementally. We in the business world – to date – rarely show such discipline.

A framework for success

This book has been written very simply to convey a concept which will help remove the mystique of successfully managing change. A visual representation of the framework described in this book appears on pages 18 and 19. You might find it helpful to keep flicking back to this illustration or even take a copy to keep to hand as you go through your change process. The framework is simple, but simple doesn't mean easy. There are many levels of detail below the surface. During any change process, things will hit you from left of field, directives will be issued over which you have no control, events and situations will occur of which you had no prior warning. Your appetite for change will sometimes be very low and your confidence will experience inevitable setbacks. This is the real world, after all. Applying the framework in this book will give you a harness, a touchstone which you can use to help you make decisions; even when the going gets tough, it will allow you to manage the change process regardless of what hits you. It will help you to structure your thoughts in such a way that you have the confidence to review progress, change behaviour, alter direction, engage stakeholders and deliver benefits time after time. Will it take away the pain completely? No. Will it increase your chances of success? Yes, considerably.

So take a quick look at the framework overleaf, then clear your mind, put away your preconceptions and let me tell you the story of Zircon.

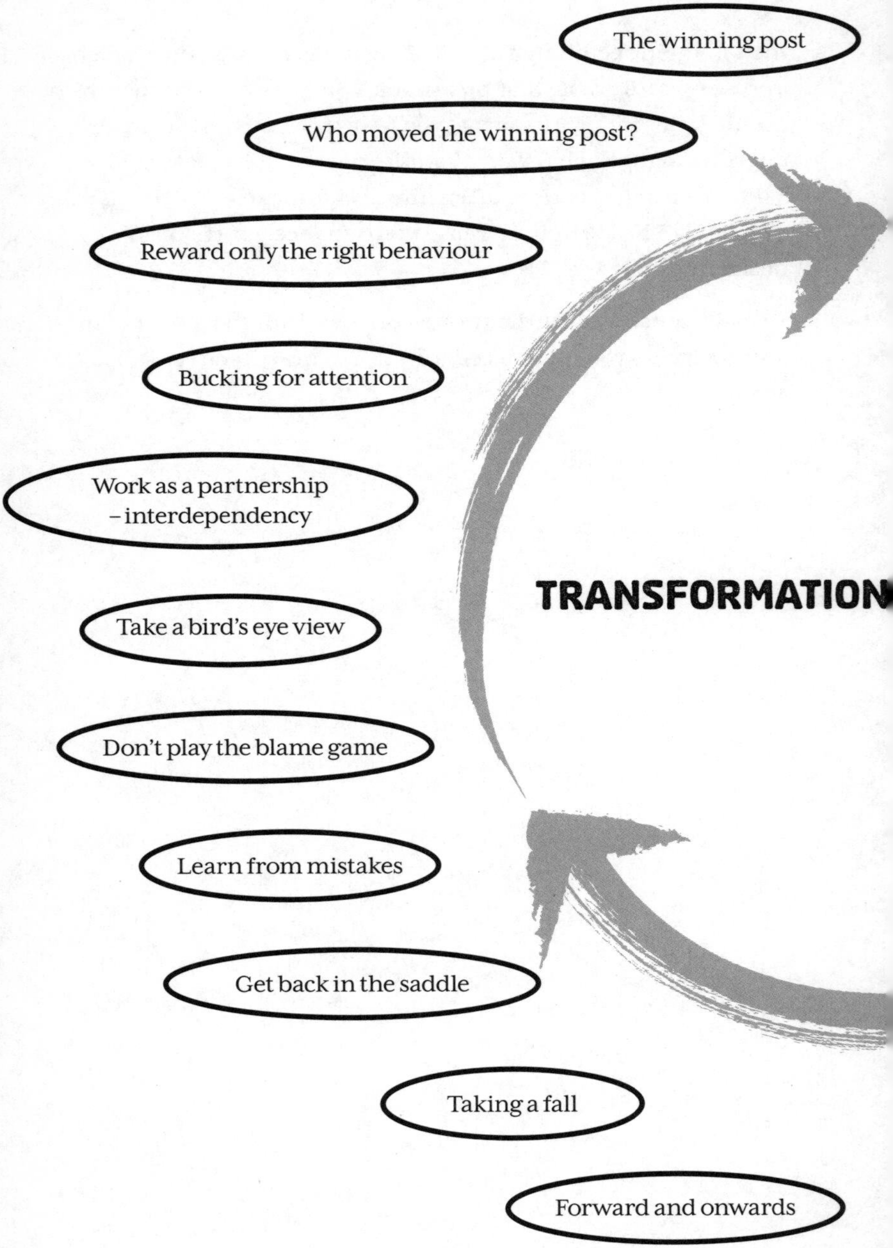

The winning post

Who moved the winning post?

Reward only the right behaviour

Bucking for attention

Work as a partnership
– interdependency

Take a bird's eye view

Don't play the blame game

Learn from mistakes

Get back in the saddle

Taking a fall

Forward and onwards

TRANSFORMATION

In the beginning

Understand where you are starting from

Know where you are going

Be realistic

Engage a helping hand to realise potential

One step at a time – building on success

FRAMEWORK

Risk, what risk?

Watch the horizon

Create a happy day

Communicate, communicate...

Celebrate success

Achieve self-carriage

1 IN THE BEGINNING

At first glance you can see that Zircon is a nice horse. He has a balanced body shape, a strong wide chest and a kind eye. He is healthy if a little overweight, having been well looked after by his previous owners. Mr Rider knows that Zircon came from a kind but inexperienced home. However his new owner – who has employed Mr Rider to develop him – is a professional horse owner and expects both his horses and Mr Rider to deliver results and a return on investment. Zircon looks as though he has only been ridden occasionally, and in a very relaxed fashion, and it's clear that he has been rarely schooled as he has little muscle tone and is out of condition. He also appears to be quite naughty and lazy, indicating perhaps that he has been allowed to do as he pleases by an indulgent but well-meaning owner.

Zircon is an OK company. In terms of performance it's doing... well, OK. But only that; it could do better. It's surviving in its chosen marketplace, but only just. It's essentially well structured, in that it has the right departments in place – but not necessarily the right balance between the departments nor the best practices and processes. All of the constituent parts don't seem to be working well together; it has potential but there is something slightly ungainly about it. Zircon isn't forward looking. Quite often it encounters obstacles and situations, both internally and externally, that it is unprepared for and therefore finds it difficult to cope with – but it does nothing in the hope that things will work out anyway. Zircon has a generally downbeat feel. It lacks momentum. It lacks spark. It's falling behind the competition, and it knows it.

But things are about to change. Zircon has a new leader, Mr Rider.

Mr Rider has plans for Zircon. He wants it to become more efficient, more balanced, more agile, more of a player in its chosen marketplace. He wants it to shine.

2 UNDERSTAND WHERE YOU ARE STARTING FROM

From his initial analysis Mr Rider can see that Zircon hasn't been well trained, but he has natural movement and great bone structure (conformation). When looking at him move, Mr Rider sees that the horse has a tendency not to do more than he has to. This is on the positive side, in a funny way, and can be worked to Mr Rider's advantage

during training; it's much easier to get a horse fit and teach it to go forward in a balanced fashion than it is having to hold back an unfit horse that just wants to plough forwards regardless. As a result of his lack of fitness, Zircon doesn't lift his back legs up off the ground properly which means that his stomach muscles are weak and hamper his ability to move forward quickly and efficiently. Work will have to be done on getting his stomach muscles to work properly, something which will take time and training.

Mr Rider appraises Zircon Ltd. He needs to know what he is dealing with. What's good? What's mediocre? What's bad? What parts of the business operate well together? What parts operate in isolation? What are the good habits that need to be nurtured? What are the bad habits that need to be replaced? He needs to gauge Zircon Ltd's potential, tune into the mood of the business and its appetite for change. And he needs to do it quickly, in a matter of a couple of months, so that he can support Zircon moving forward in the most efficient and effective way.

Mr Rider also knows that he needs to understand Zircon Ltd's past, its history, what made it into what it is today. Has past leadership been strong, and does the business already have good foundations in place for the future? Or has it been allowed to fall behind the times, to get slow and cumbersome? Have its customers' needs remained static or have they changed dramatically? The past will give an insight into why Zircon operates in the way it does, and will also allow him to understand the best way to set about changing it. Understanding the past will also allow him to identify with Zircon Ltd more easily.

A nervous air fills the business. The new leader doesn't know anything about the company, what it has been through, what it has had to put up with. He doesn't know the things that it did really well in years gone by – before the market changed, before money got tight. What if the new leader doesn't do things in the same way as the old leader, or doesn't want them done that way? As a company, Zircon Ltd doesn't know if it can do things any differently. To be honest, it isn't even sure it wants to. It doesn't want to lose its past; it's been fun. The business is frightened of change, it likes operating how it is – in short, it feels OK. Comfy, in fact. The ambiguity surrounding future direction is now making Zircon Ltd an unsettling place to be.

* **TIP:** *Examine the past to inform the future and listen to what is going on.*

It makes sense to examine a company's history in a number of ways. Look at the trends, the history of the business or department you are looking to change. Where did it start from – what need or gap in the market did it address/fulfil? How have market conditions and customer needs changed over the years? What has the financial landscape been – are margins fluctuating and what trends are

apparent? How have client needs changed over the years? Has leadership been strong and what has the leadership style been like? Has the business ever demonstrated a capability to change in the past? How is performance measured – and is it measured appropriately?

Once you have done this, you can then bring things up to date by looking at the 'as-is state' – where the business/department is now:

- Is the business cash rich?
- Are shareholders/stakeholders supportive/effective?
- Which parts of the business operate efficiently?
- Which parts of the business are performing poorly?
- How do customers (external and internal) view the service they are given?
- What is the brand position in the marketplace?
- Does the proposition reflect customer needs?
- Are the senior managers united in a common vision/goal?
- Are employees aligned to this common vision/goal?
- To what extent does the business look forward?
- Is there a strong pipeline of new opportunities and products?

Take a systemic approach and look across the whole organisation – how each part impacts upon the others. What capabilities does the organisation have, and does it have the right people in the right roles? Who are the talented people in the organisation and how are they being managed and developed?

And, of course, listen. Talk to the senior managers of the business individually and get their take on the situation; talk to employees and ask them what works and what doesn't – what would they do differently? Talk to clients about their experience of working with you. Would they recommend you to someone else in their network? Gain an understanding of what clients and key stakeholders (external or internal) are looking for.

3 KNOW WHERE YOU ARE GOING

Zircon has a strong jump although he sometimes loses concentration, which means that he isn't always concentrating on the job in hand and that each piece of his body doesn't always work together to produce the optimum result. But when everything does work together his jump has huge scope and potential. His movement is very balanced so would lend itself well to dressage, although possibly not at the highest level. However, he absolutely adores cross country; he has great speed and is fearless and brave when confronted by the most daunting of cross-country jumps. Weighing up the facts, and given Zircon's all-round ability, Mr Rider decides to focus Zircon on an Olympic sport, three-day eventing. The first day is a dressage test; the second day is a timed cross-country round with time penalties. On the third day horses and riders enter a round of

show jumping over coloured poles. The three-day event was modelled on the need for cavalry officers to fight in battle and negotiate a long, hard-run battlefield race, including clearing fences and obstacles. Requiring practically every known skill and plenty of endurance, a three-day event asks a lot of both horse and rider. Mr Rider knew that this would play to Zircon's strengths as eventing spans all of the disciplines, but without the need to be at an international standard in all three (similar to a human triathlon). Mr Rider now has the ultimate vision of competing with Zircon and winning at international competitions.

Mr Rider knows that without a clear view of where Zircon Ltd is going, the company stands little chance of getting there.

Having appraised the business, Mr Rider thinks long and hard about his vision for it. This vision needs to be challenging, potentially achievable and allow Zircon Ltd to shine in its chosen arena. Just as importantly, it must address the needs of all stakeholders.

Taking his initial analysis of the business and the potential he feels it has, he then takes feedback from across Zircon. He talks extensively with Zircon's senior managers and employees, he reviews client needs, the external marketplace and the competition it faces. He reviews the arenas that are open to the business and identifies a number of potential options. Then, following further analysis and consultation, he whittles it down to the one arena in which he feels Zircon will do best, one which will play to its strengths and where he believes, with work, it can outperform the competition. An arena where it can be number one, where Zircon Ltd can set the pace, create new standards and ways of working.

Next, he engages his senior managers to look at how long the transformation will take and what it will cost. The senior managers

do the work but there is resistance; they find the idea of change unsettling. With this information to hand they then analyse the return on investment, assuming Zircon achieves the vision. They add into the mix the risks as they currently are, and the actions and associated costs that will need to be taken in order to mitigate them.

As his vision is formulated, Mr Rider keeps his senior stakeholders informed and engaged. It is important that he takes them on the journey with him and that they understand his thinking and have the opportunity to point out issues and pitfalls as things develop so that they can become supportive of the proposed changes and plans.

However, every department across Zircon Ltd feels wary, very wary, and slightly afraid. It doesn't feel good to be scrutinised, to be judged and not to know why. Every part of the business feels tense. It's sitting in the middle of a pregnant pause and knows it. Something is going to happen – the question is when.

* TIP: *acknowledge uncertainty and deal with it openly.*

To understand where you want to go to it is important that you analyse the facts you have gathered to date from a high-level perspective; don't fall into the 'analysis paralysis' trap. Identify strengths, weaknesses, opportunities and threats (SWOT analysis), and analyse the marketplace and where it is heading – use trusted third parties to provide another view. Gain an understanding of how the business/department is running from a cost basis and benchmark this against similar organisations, and identify options in consultation with the relevant stakeholders.

Then do a detailed gap analysis of all the options – where the business is now and where you want it to be. Consider the following:

- Competitive analysis – where are you positioned in the market? Is this the right place for you?
- Does the company have the talent required to get to where it needs to be?
- Does it have the systems and processes needed to be successful?
- What kind of operating structure is right for the company in its chosen market position?
- Can you afford to make this change? Will it generate the returns shareholders are looking for?
- What are the timescales in which this change needs to deliver those returns?

And, having analysed all of the facts, identify the strongest option – the vision.

4 BE REALISTIC

Watching Zircon negotiating the fences on his own, without the hindrance of a rider, allows Mr Rider to get to know how clever Zircon is and assess his sense of self-preservation and his natural style and ability. Zircon is bold, which will stand him in good stead. However, there is a certain stiffness that prevents his hind legs getting far enough forward under him in order to provide sufficient power for the jump, but further flat work can help to overcome this. His hoofs are also quite brittle and look as though they break easily. A good farrier and foot supplement should help address this, but his feet are always going to be a weak spot and will need special care. Zircon also finds it difficult to naturally shorten his stride and jump from a deep spot – something Mr Rider will need to take into account, adjusting his riding style accordingly. Most important of all, however, Zircon displays a desire to learn and that is really positive.

Having identified a vision for Zircon Ltd, Mr Rider sets about proving that it's an achievable one.

He assesses what needs to change in the short term, in the medium term and in the longer term and, very importantly, is realistic about what he is not going to be able to change but will just have to work around. He prioritises what needs to change, identifying those things which, when done, will deliver most benefit. He puts them at the top of the list.

With the business and its senior managers, he works on developing a very clear picture of how Zircon Ltd will need to look, need to feel and need to operate in order to achieve this vision. He knows that it's no good having some parts working brilliantly while others are underperforming. Such a situation would just hamper the business from developing in a balanced way. The bottom line is that every part of the business must perform to its optimum and clarity is needed around what everyone needs to do in order to achieve this.

This work takes time. Not all parts of the business are as helpful as others; a lot of difficult questions are being asked of Zircon Ltd and, in many quarters, there is a general lack of understanding of the need to change. The period of initial engagement is never going to be easy, but Mr Rider knows that it cannot be rushed. He also recognises that certain people may never become aligned and that at some point hard decisions relating to them will need to be made.

Once all this work is complete Mr Rider takes a reality check. He knows that changing behaviours, changing habits, changing the way things are done so that they become second nature takes much longer than either he or the business would like to think. By setting unrealistic timescales he could also be setting the business up for failure, so Mr Rider and his senior managers do a realistic review of timings. They factor in more time and redo their calculations. They set themselves up for success. They also identify any quick wins which may have become evident from the analysis, those

things that could be changed quickly and easily but could also begin to create positive change within the organisation. Only when Mr Rider and his senior managers believe that everything stacks up – then, and only then – does Mr Rider commit himself and Zircon Ltd to progressing the vision and its achievement.

To avoid ambiguity he articulates the vision clearly to everyone, setting both Zircon Ltd and himself up for success.

* **TIP:** *What is in your gift? What will you be able to change and what will you just have to work around? Know what you want to achieve; be realistic about money, timing and resources and consider how to describe it to the people in your business in a compelling vision.*

To make a compelling vision, stakeholders need to believe that it is achievable and that all the due diligence has been done before arriving at it. To ensure that this is the case, first undertake a capability analysis. Then assess both team and individual capabilities. What capabilities do you need, and what capabilities have you already got? Can the gap be bridged through training and/or development? If so, is the timescale for such training or development realistic within the period in which returns on the change will be expected? Is there a need to buy in new talent, and is such talent available at a price you can afford? Has time been allowed for the learning curve of any new people? Finally, how much will the people change cost? Does this still stack up against the case you outlined in the vision?

Then take a look at the financials. How much investment is required – and how much investment is available? How will performance measures be impacted?

Now look at the impact on your clients. Will delivery suffer? Are clients likely to be lost? Will there be an impact on the pipeline – and if so, at what cost? Think about whether you should be looking for new or different clients. What are the benefits to your clients, and will any of them be immediate benefits? Will your brand be impacted?

Then, once all of this has been done, assess the operational impact of your vision. Will operations be impacted? What will the impact on technology be? What are the costs and/or timescale implications? Will your head count need to be increased or maybe decreased?

Work with your senior team to agree a clear articulation of the vision which can be used across the business or department. Develop a communication strategy and plan, and ensure that sufficient funds are available to implement it.

5 ENGAGE A HELPING HAND TO REALISE POTENTIAL

Mr Rider knew that he would need expert help in developing Zircon. This wasn't about him lacking confidence in his knowledge and abilities, but more about recognising the fact that others — especially those looking from the outside in an unemotional way — could add immense value and insight and encourage new ways of approaching potential issues. He was a generalist and looked at the animal as a whole, but would need to also bring in specialists in order to develop certain enhanced capabilities in both Zircon and himself with regard to the nuances of the three disciplines of dressage, cross country and show jumping. Yes, it would be essential at certain times to have a second pair of eyes and an objective sounding board for his thoughts and ideas.

At Zircon Ltd, Mr Rider is very confident in his skills and abilities; however, he realises that neither he nor the business knows everything. For Zircon to develop correctly, and for the business to realise its full potential, he is only too aware that both he and the business will need help with hard and soft skills.

He commits from day one to bringing in expert support, and Coach Ltd is engaged. Coach provides a broad range of skills which can be tapped into as and when needed, and will provide him and Zircon with an impartial sounding board for their thoughts and ideas. It will question, challenge and coach, and help them achieve the level

of clarity and objectivity that they will need if the business is to develop effectively. Additionally, in the short term, Coach will help fill gaps in Mr Rider and Zircon Ltd's skills base and experience, while in the longer term it will hand on new skills and help to develop new ways of thinking, working and problem solving. However, in engaging Coach, Mr Rider will not forget that achieving at the end of the day is down to him and the business – and to the strength of their partnership. Neither can achieve everything alone. Coach is there to help accelerate progress and learning, not to do the job for them.

* TIP: *Don't think you can effect change alone. Identify areas in which you will need help and support.*

In the very beginning it is wise to identify a business coach who can help you, the leader, on your personal journey.

Consider whether you will need help effecting change in the form of project management. What internal mechanisms/processes do you have already for managing change? How are projects controlled within your organisation? Do you, as a leader, have real-time visibility over the status of key projects and initiatives? You also need to identify external organisations who can help support you in handing on new skills and ways of working, and analyse the cost of employing these organisations.

Once you have done that you can move on. Using the skills analysis you have already performed to guide you, identify external resources who can help you find the best external talent. Put your best people in the team to show commitment to the importance of the change project and its chance of success, while also working to identify internal stars who can help champion and drive the change.

6 ONE STEP AT A TIME – BUILDING ON SUCCESS

Mr Rider first identified the work which would deliver the maximum benefit to Zircon. He decided they would first work to get Zircon to use and control his powerful back end while relaxing over the top of his body without tensing (a bit like a back stretch in Pilates). Although this is something that horses don't do in the wild, achieving it would mean that Zircon would be more agile and comfortable when carrying Mr Rider on his back. Focusing on the one thing that would create the most significant positive difference in Zircon would mean that a lot of the other changes thought to be needed in the beginning might well disappear – they would occur naturally, without effort. It would also give Zircon a positive experience of change and its equally positive benefits.

With all thoughts firmly fixed on the achievement of the vision, a strategy and plan is prepared at Zircon Ltd. The strategy is kept short and simple to aid understanding and execution, and the plan is broken down into goals (benefits) and specific action steps which will support the achievement of each goal. Stringent indicators are attached to each goal to allow for success to be accurately gauged, monitored and measured.

Mr Rider knows what needs to change. However, he also knows that if he is to increase the probability of himself and the business both achieving and getting maximum benefit from the achievement of

each goal, only one goal should be focused on at a time. He works with the different parts of Zircon Ltd to identify the specific goals which will deliver the maximum benefits, and the optimum order in which they should be approached.

The first goal for the business will be that which will provide the greatest benefit and have the biggest impact on the way it operates. Its achievement will create significant positive changes within the business operationally, but also in its belief in its ability to change (and change for the better) and its level of confidence. It will provide a return on investment and give the business a strong foundation for future growth. The first level of trust between the business and the leader will have been developed.

Having established a foundation, Mr Rider's strategy is to make things feel incrementally better, allowing the change process to gain its own momentum built on confidence and success.

All parts of the business can feel that something is about to happen – but what? No one's told them at the sharp end, and all this talk about vision... what's that all about? What's happening to jobs? Will there be redundancies? Should they go? Should they stay? It's unnerving.

* **TIP:** *Don't take a scatter-gun approach to change. Focus on the one thing which will have the most positive effect. Achieve one goal at a time. By taking this approach, many of the changes you initially thought needed to happen may no longer be necessary. Goals, when individually focused on, can usually be more easily and cohesively achieved – and their successful achievement will promote energy, learning and confidence within the organisation.*

To ensure you pick the right thing to focus on, first identify what the business is doing well and what you would wish it to keep doing. Promote these as part of your communications plan, and highlight them in your performance reviews of senior managers. Have them do the same with their teams.

What needs to be done differently within the business in order to achieve the vision? Distil these into some key change messages and highlight them as part of your communications plan. Include the change behaviours in key performance indicators (KPIs) for senior managers, then look at what other steps need to be taken to change those things in your:

- Processes;
- Systems;
- Organisation structure;
- Branding;
- Marketing.

Don't forget to distinguish between those changes which must happen and those changes which are just nice to have!

Then do a cost/benefit analysis of all the changes you have identified and an analysis of all the necessary changes. Identify that change which will create the biggest positive impact and which plays to the strengths of your business.

In addition, use an independent person (potentially a coach) to challenge your thoughts and assumptions and to help validate your thinking, and create a road map of changes. Validate this road map with your senior managers.

7 RISK, WHAT RISK?

Mr Rider knows that he must listen to and work with Zircon if he is to avoid pushing him too far, too soon and risk causing injury and depression. He must nurture Zircon's understanding and interest in doing the job. There is a risk in his own and Zircon's owner's haste to realise the horse's potential: he might spoil what he started with by doing everything too quickly and progressing to the next stage before the previous one had been embedded. Mr Rider appreciates that it takes time to replace old ways of doing things with new ones, and knows he will have to do many repetitions until Zircon understands what *he is asking. He also knows from exercising his own body that muscles don't just accept new ways of doing things overnight – they go to it kicking and screaming.*

Mr Rider firmly believes that without a clear view of the potential obstacles to success at Zircon Ltd, there is little chance of getting out of the starting blocks.

Now in possession of the draft plan, he and Coach consult across the business to gain an understanding of the possible risks to delivering change. Rather than feeling fazed by having a clear and accurate picture of the risks, Mr Rider feels confident. He and the business amend the plan to mitigate the risks that have been identified and are now sure that the timescales and action steps which shape the plan are realistic and achievable.

But Mr Rider is even more realistic; he knows he cannot foresee all the risks at this stage in the game. So, to mitigate the inevitable but unforeseen risks, he takes the decision that Zircon Ltd will progress to the achievement of each goal only when the previous one has been successfully achieved. Additionally, he makes the commitment to listen acutely to what he is told and pay close attention to what he sees. If he believes that any part of the business is not sufficiently prepared to successfully complete a goal within the plan's timeframe, he will step back, re-evaluate the situation, assess what is wrong and then repeat activities or provide additional training or coaching where necessary. The business will move forward towards the completion of the goal once, and only once, these additional things have been achieved.

If need be, deadlines will be changed. They will be driven by successful delivery of benefits – to the business, to clients, to shareholders – and not by timings artificially put on plans. Mr Rider is aware that there will be pressure on them from stakeholders to

keep to plans, but he is confident that their benefits' delivery record will speak for itself and allow him to engage stakeholders should any change in timings prove necessary. It won't always be easy to convince them, but he will stick to his guns. He will be absolutely sure that the business will be fit for purpose for each new step it takes.

* **TIP:** *Understand your potential risks and make allowance for their occurrence within the plan. Don't be tempted to become a slave to the timings on a plan. Only progress towards a goal once the previous goal has been completed. Monitor potential risks as an ongoing process.*

There are several things you can do to help you manage both risks and your stakeholders' reaction to any remedial action you may need to take should they occur. When first engaging stakeholders, make it clear that there must be flexibility within the plan for unforeseen circumstances – and that allowing for changes to the plan where necessary is a strength which will ultimately support and speed successful delivery, and not a weakness.

Then undertake a risk analysis, identifying and evaluating potential risks, looking at:
- Probability;
- Potential cost impact;
- Timescales;
- People implications;
- Customer implications.

Allocate responsibility and accountability for tracking possible risks and initiating preventative or remedial action where appropriate and for monitoring the external environment, especially in respect to competitor activity. Revisit the plan with your senior team and ensure that it is realistic, and use your coach to challenge you as to whether your risk assessments are honest (no rose-tinted glasses, mind!).

8 WATCH THE HORIZON

The news was just out that the latest version of three-day eventing was to be the short course, which eliminates portions of the course in the interests of saving space, time and wear and tear on the horse. The new short form was to omit the steeplechase. This change had been expected for some time, as creating the short form allowed eventing to keep its place in the Olympics; it had been in danger of being lost because it required so much space. The short form three-day event *would require more intensive, shorter bursts of speed and thus needed a different type of stamina. This meant that Zircon's training would need to be changed to focus more on agility and less on endurance.*

As each goal at Zircon Ltd is achieved, Mr Rider and Coach will review progress. They will, with input from the business, review both internal and external dynamics to pick up any subtle changes in climate. This exercise will allow them to judge whether the direction which has been set for Zircon Ltd is still the best one. They are confident that by doing this they will be able to pick up any changes in the business's operating environment before they become major issues, and change their goals to address them accordingly. This will allow both Mr Rider and the business to become much more agile, setting the organisation up for success and creating the momentum for future cultural change.

Mr Rider is confident that he can engage his stakeholders' commitment to the changes to the original plan. Because of this, he is not fazed about their potential reactions and does not allow that to affect his decision-making process. He knows that as Zircon Ltd achieves each goal (benefit), their trust and confidence in him as a leader will grow too.

At any given stage in the process Mr Rider is confident that he will know where each part of the business is in its development, what progress they are making and what they need to do next to take them forward to success.

* **TIP:** *Keep an eye on progress, including what is happening externally, so that you are well placed to make any adjustments to plans/direction which may be necessary.*

It helps to put processes in place to ensure that your finger is on the pulse, so set up review parameters. Consider key performance indicators (KPIs):

- Financials, including key metrics from the business case for the change.
- People metrics, e.g. attrition, annual people survey results.
- Operational indicators on key internal processes.

Also keep an eye on the external factors – such as the environment (political and economic) or new technology and its potential use by competitors.

Allocate responsibility for initiating a review and driving forward any actions which come out of it, and ask for honest and open feedback from business stakeholders, putting in place processes to ensure this happens regularly. But be careful not to bog decision-making down in bureaucracy; create a smooth, effective process for decision-making and action-taking instead.

Don't fall in love with your vision, either; be open to changing it for the better. Use a coach to challenge the currency of your vision. Is it still the right one? And, as always, communicate any changes and the reason for them clearly to all stakeholders, paying particular attention to the different needs of the individual stakeholders concerned.

9 CREATE A HAPPY DAY

No one works at their best when they feel unhappy, vulnerable or unsure of what they are supposed to be doing. Mr Rider knows that this is equally true for horses, so from the outset he stays in harmony with Zircon; he listens to the horse's needs and mood and keeps his instructions clear, consistent and balanced. When on Zircon's back, Mr Rider notes every pattern of movement and stays in rhythm, giving only the subtlest of direction when required. As a result, Zircon is happy and confident in his work and is praised for his efforts. Praise gives Zircon a lovely warm feeling; it makes him happy to know that he is doing well.

Zircon Ltd feels unsettled. Nothing feels good. It feels as though it's been in a pregnant pause forever. Every part of it feels unsure of what it should be doing. It wants to stay where it is. It certainly doesn't feel confident about moving forward. It doesn't even know if it can move forward. Forward, where's forward?

Mr Rider takes up the reins. Up until now he has stood to one side, looking, listening and appraising. Now he must lead.

He feels the mood of the organisation. He acknowledges that any change will feel uncomfortable, particularly in the beginning but also at other stages when things become difficult. That's OK, that's natural. But he does know that nothing will move forward unless he removes the fear – the fear of the unknown, the fear of getting things wrong, the fear of failure. He certainly doesn't perform at his best when he feels scared, anxious and unsure. Why should the people in the business be any different?

Of one thing he is certain: his leadership will be marked by the positive nature in which things are approached and achieved. If progress is to be made it has to be a win/win situation: a win for the business and the people within it, and a win for himself. He, as leader, will at no stage make any part of Zircon Ltd feel that it is being asked to do something which is too difficult or for which it is not sufficiently prepared or qualified. And he will praise even the smallest amount of progress, and do so often. He will strive to make Zircon a happy place to be.

* TIP: *Remove the fear, especially of failure and its associated repercussions. People want to be happy in their work so strive to make this possible in a realistic way.*

There are a number of things you can do to help create a positive environment:

- Coach your senior managers in how to manage successful change. Empower them to take their own decisions and take responsibility for making things happen and overcoming obstacles, and encourage them to coach and nurture their own staff. Encourage them to lead by example and to take tough decisions and manage them with integrity.
- Unblock obstacles which threaten to hamper progress.
- Listen actively to feedback and take positive action where necessary.
- Recognise limitations and give support to overcome them.
- Reward and recognise good work/progress – celebrate success often.
- Don't allow one area/person to have too much of a negative influence.
- Ensure all interventions are well timed and well judged – learn the art of effective brokering.

10 COMMUNICATE, COMMUNICATE...

Mr Rider wants to canter around the school and so repeats the instructions and training he and Zircon have practised for so long. He sits deeper in the saddle and puts his inside leg on the girth and outside leg slightly behind the girth (the girth is a broad strap attached to the saddle, going under the horse's belly; it must be fastened tightly as it is what holds the saddle on the horse's back) and sends Zircon forward. Zircon understands what he is asking for; it is being asked for clearly and consistently, and he has practised it many times with Mr Rider. He responds positively and happily. He engages his hind legs and softens along the top of his body, giving Mr Rider a balanced, forward-going canter.

Mr Rider's priority as the leader at Zircon Ltd is to remove the uncertainty and create a strong partnership with the business. To do this he must communicate clearly and effectively. He must explain and demonstrate what he expects both collectively and individually from each part of Zircon Ltd and, in turn, make very clear what the business can expect from him. He must be consistent in how he behaves and how he asks for things to be done. The business and its people must know what they're expected to do, when and why. Communication is a two-way process and people within the business must learn to communicate openly and constructively as well; Mr Rider isn't a mind reader, after all. Ambiguity will only hamper forward movement and create frustration, so there must be no ambiguity.

Work begins on the action steps towards the achievement of the first goal. This goal has been chosen to play to the business's strengths and is aimed at delivering a positive result quickly. Mr Rider starts off as he means to continue. He is very clear about what he wants to achieve and communicates this across the business. He is consistent in what he asks from the various parts of the business both individually and collectively, and in how he asks for it. He listens to the messages he is getting from Zircon Ltd and he praises positive activity frequently, no matter how small the achievement is. Confidence and understanding builds. As the business progresses towards achieving the first goal, he constantly listens to and acts upon feedback across the organisation, accurately monitoring progress and adjusting support and training according to the need of each individual part.

Zircon Ltd feels a bit better. Well, some parts feel a bit better; others are confused and some are even trying to carry on as before. Never mind; at least Mr Rider is taking charge. At least something is happening; the business will just do what it's told – most of the time, and if it's easy; if it's difficult – well, that might be another matter. And it's being told when things have been done well, which is nice

and makes it feel more confident. An ideal situation, really; success and no responsibility. Not sure about communicating, though...

* TIP: *Silence is leaden, not golden, when trying to bring about change.*

So that you don't fall into the poor communication trap, ensure that you view communication as a continuous conversation with stakeholders. Be clear with them about when they can expect to hear from you and by which channels; set out a road map of communications and establish some clear touch points, e.g. a weekly email from the leadership team.

Make sure you're always clear about what you want your audience to know, feel, think, do and behave as a result of any communication. Incrementally build understanding of the evolving situation through communications and engagement, using two-way lines of communication which are open and nurtured. Don't forget to ensure that communication has integrity and is unambiguous.

Make everyone responsible for good communications; at the same time make sure your senior managers are speaking from the same page and that messages are consistent. Get out and about and talk with people and encourage your managers to do the same. Don't avoid communicating bad news, but ensure you communicate it in a balanced way which also addresses how you are going to overcome the setback.

And listen to the communication you receive. If you receive feedback or challenges make sure you address the points raised; simply acknowledging comment/feedback is not sufficient. Finally, don't forget that your body language speaks volumes!

11 CELEBRATE SUCCESS

Zircon had really enjoyed himself. He'd jumped all the fences without knocking one down or hitting his legs on the poles; he'd had fun and knew, by the praise he'd received from Mr Rider and his owner, and by the applause from the crowd, that he had done really well on completion of the jumping course. The carrots and apples in his feed were greatly appreciated, too!

The first goal has been achieved. Things are feeling a bit better across Zircon Ltd already. It feels better moving forward; freer, somehow. The business is still not quite used to doing things the new way but that seems to get easier with practice; it's certainly much more comfortable than when it was gripped by the fear of the unknown, just waiting for something bad to happen. Yes, it feels better – not perfect, but better.

Achieving the first goal successfully has certainly improved confidence across the organisation. It seems to be functioning better, too. Maybe it could change (the jury is still out) but the praise makes it feel good. It feels great to achieve something and for the achievement to be recognised. Mr Rider did well – this time. Maybe he is someone people within Zircon Ltd might grow to trust… only might, mind.

Mr Rider feels a subtle difference across Zircon. It feels more supple, somehow; the occasions when every part is working together are becoming more frequent. There's still a long way to go, but it's good to start feeling the potential come alive.

* **TIP:** *Thank you and well done cost nothing.*

Praise is a very simple thing (and gives a great return) but is quite often forgotten when pressure of work gets the better of us. To prevent this from happening in your organisation make sure you get into the habit of recognising positive achievements no matter how small, and articulating the benefits of each achievement. Praise frequently but not insincerely, and don't forget to say 'thank you'. Recognise and encourage the right behaviours in your senior management team, and lead by example.

Do something that marks or celebrates success if the budget allows. This doesn't have to be elaborate; even something as simple as mid-afternoon cakes can work wonders. However, only allow a small pause to celebrate success and then ensure that the organisation maintains its momentum; people have a tendency to lose urgency once they see that things are going in the right direction. So remind them of the vision and goals you are shooting for, highlight how far you have come and what the next milestone to celebrate will be.

12 ACHIEVE SELF-CARRIAGE

Mr Rider decides on a different approach; he knows that up until now he has been taking responsibility for everything. He has constantly been telling Zircon when to take off to achieve a jump or when to straighten his body for a more balanced landing. By now, with all the training and practice he had done, Zircon should have learned what to do himself. Mr Rider realises that Zircon is relying on his instructions and following them blindly, taking no responsibility for looking where he is going or for overcoming an obstacle (a jump). Mr Rider metaphorically stands back; he sets the direction they are to go in and then leaves Zircon to do the rest. This requires practice and some errors are made while Zircon learns to do this, but the jumps do become easier when he concentrates on

the task in hand, looks forward to where he is going and takes
responsibility for how he carries his own body when jumping
the fence.

Together, Zircon Ltd and Mr Rider have achieved the first goal. It felt good. Now, forward and onwards to the second.

As things progress, different parts of the company are being asked to do a few things which don't come quite so easily. The business doesn't really like change and some of the things it's being asked to do don't really feel comfortable at all. Some parts, particularly, have made their views known rather vocally. No matter; with luck, things will eventually return to how they were. In any event the various parts of the business will continue to do what they are asked to do – if it's easy to do so. If it's not, why bother?

Mr Rider is frustrated with how the business is performing. It doesn't seem to be working with him; it's behaving like a passenger.

The various parts of the business aren't working together seamlessly enough, nor are they taking sufficient responsibility for themselves or how they perform. This situation needs to change. The collective parts of the business must work together and work things out for themselves. Zircon Ltd must take responsibility for its own success or failure. In short, the business must learn to carry itself.

As the leader, Mr Rider is very clear about his role – to lead the business. His ultimate aim is to set direction but to interfere in the day-to-day running of the company as little as possible. He is there to help the business establish itself in such a way that it is balanced, agile and forward moving, able to cope confidently with anything which may be thrown at it. In short, his role is to set the business up for success, and the rest is the business's job.

Things are subtly beginning to change within Zircon Ltd. Mr Rider is still very clear about what he wants and how he asks for it. However, where obstacles arise – obstacles which he knows the organisation has the internal capabilities to deal with – he waits for the business to work out how to overcome them. Mr Rider will coach Zircon Ltd or hand on new skills if they are needed if he is told about them; but doing the doing is definitely down to the business.

Zircon Ltd is not sure that it likes this turn of events. Having no responsibility was good; this being empowered lark can be hard work. It's not something the business is used to. On the positive side Zircon is beginning to feel more agile, not that it would let on. Each obstacle it overcomes makes it braver, takes it a little further forward.

* **TIP:** *The business and its constituents have a responsibility to help the business as a whole achieve its goals. Empower people to do their bit and work at creating an adult-to-adult relationship with stakeholders across the business as opposed to that of a parent and child.*

The following will help you in defining responsibilities and establishing a relationship of shared responsibility:

- Be very clear about what the achievement of the goal you are aiming for looks and feels like.
- Clearly articulate the performance contract – what everyone's role/responsibility is.
- Communicate what you expect to be achieved and who is responsible for what.
- Sponsor and reward a culture of collaboration, teamwork and ownership.
- Stand back – don't be tempted to interfere unnecessarily.
- Allow people to recognise, acknowledge and learn from their mistakes.
- When asked for help, coach the asker to allow them to find a solution for themselves; don't be tempted to 'tell' or 'instruct' unless absolutely essential.

Finally, lead by example – especially where your senior management team are concerned. See if progress is comparable across all areas of the business, and be prepared at this point to undertake any difficult conversations that may be needed with senior managers if their areas are not keeping up with the changes needed. Identify any blockers and encourage the managers to eliminate them – and be prepared to evaluate whether the senior team is still the right one to take the business forward.

13 FORWARD AND ONWARDS

Zircon spent a long time not wanting to move forward, wanting to stay as he was and only put the minimum of effort into things — but this quite often resulted in him putting more effort into not achieving anything and feeling really quite vulnerable. With Mr Rider's help Zircon now accepts that impulsion makes him stronger, more in control, more agile. When show jumping, impulsion really carries Zircon over the fences; in dressage, it elevates him and allows him to make the more complex moves. Zircon spots his fence from far away and his enthusiasm, impulsion and power helps him soar beautifully over it.

At Zircon Ltd, things move forward, goals are achieved, the benefits of the change are beginning to be felt and stakeholders' expectations are managed.

The business is looking forward. Zircon Ltd is actively moving forward; it has impulsion. It's funny, now that it's starting to look where it's going and move towards change, how things are becoming so much easier to deal with. Being able to anticipate potential obstacles gives the organisation greater control of how

it moves forward – removes the fear, in fact. Consciously moving forward and controlling how it moves and where it moves to definitely feels much nicer than the tight, knotted feeling it used to get from trying to stand still.

If the business is honest, before Mr Rider came on board things always changed around it even if it didn't change, and because it wasn't looking it just had to react. It had to deal with things it didn't want to, hadn't planned to. And then, because it was reacting and different parts of it reacted in different ways, it didn't always do the smartest thing. Working collectively, and looking and actively moving forward, gives it more control, more flexibility. It can choose its own path. After all, things are less scary when you can see them coming and decide how you will approach them.

Confidence is growing. Everything feels more fluid. Change has started to gather its own momentum. There are obviously still some major hurdles to overcome and the bad days are only just starting to be outnumbered by the good ones – but with Mr Rider's leadership, and the new skills and new ways of working that have been acquired across the board at Zircon Ltd, things are looking good.

* TIP: *Keep the momentum going – moving backwards or standing still is not an option!*

When you start to pick up momentum:
- Enjoy!
- Acknowledge what has been achieved and celebrate success.
- Reflect.
- Keep a light touch.

And perhaps, if you are really brave, start to challenge yourself to set stretch goals and re-evaluate the vision. Is it bold enough? Can you be braver still? You made it this far! Perhaps involve an external coach in this to bring an outside perspective on just how successful you have been and what the future potential is.

14 TAKING A FALL

Zircon had always disliked wide, brightly coloured jumps and today was no different; they scared him. Mr Rider had not taken his dislike seriously enough and although they had had a short practice jumping them at home, there hadn't really been time to do it properly before the next scheduled competition. Mr Rider had failed to help Zircon to really overcome his dislike prior to competing – and he didn't feel ready or able to jump them, so he didn't. He refused the jump and Mr Rider fell off.

At Zircon Ltd the achievement of another goal is scheduled for ten days' time – according to the plan. Mr Rider pushes forward, keen to keep to the plan. Contrary to his original commitment, he stops listening. He doesn't want to hear what the business is telling him: that it has gaps in its skills base, that it isn't working cohesively, that it isn't confident in its own abilities, that it just isn't sufficiently ready to attempt the next goal in the specified time. As such he fails to mitigate his risks. He pushes forward, regardless.

The goal is attempted as per the timings on the plan. The business fails to successfully achieve it. Mr Rider feels shaken; Zircon Ltd feels shaken. Confidence ebbs.

Quite frankly, the business feels as though it is back at the beginning, when Mr Rider had first joined. This failure has brought all of the old fears and insecurities to the fore; everyone just knew this change would bring no good. Enough people told Mr Rider the business wasn't ready – and that says a lot for communication, doesn't it? All the individual parts of the business had even begun to trust one another and work together, but now... well, each part had their own beef about the failure. And as for Mr Rider's leadership? He was just beginning to be trusted, but why would you now?

Doubting his own ability was not a common occurrence for Mr Rider, but the failure had shocked him a bit. He felt like he had fallen from a great height. He understood completely that the business was shaken, and who could blame it? His own self-belief had flagged considerably. Could he really do it, or was he kidding himself? Could he really lead this business to success?

His confidence was severely dented and his natural inclination was to retreat to his office and lick his wounds. But what would that achieve? Nothing. He knew that there were valuable lessons to be learned from this setback, ones that would establish an important reference point for the future. Being big enough and brave enough to analyse and admit what had gone wrong, put it right, move forward, learn a lesson from it and lead from the front – that was what was needed now. He knew he didn't have the objectivity to do this alone. Coach's insight, objectivity and support would once again be invaluable.

* **TIP:** *Acknowledge that setbacks wind you, but deal with them constructively.*

Practice the following to help you turn a negative into a positive:
- Recognise a setback when it happens.
- Acknowledge the setback and be honest with yourself and others about why it happened.
- Don't retreat into yourself.
- Listen to feedback but avoid becoming defensive.
- Step back and take an objective view.
- Ask for support.
- Enlist an independent party (possibly a coach) to help you with valuable self-analysis.
- Revisit the first principles of what you set out to achieve.
- Perform a root cause analysis to understand the weakness that caused this failure.
- Log lessons learned, including those things which have gone really well.
- Review your organisational structure and behaviours – are they supporting the change?
- Question whether anything changed in the external market that you might have missed.

And remember: this setback can be overcome. Pick yourself up and dust yourself down!

15 GET BACK IN THE SADDLE

Mr Rider brushes himself off and mentally puts himself in the position of leader, recognising and learning from the mistakes that had been made. He brings in a coach to support him and to provide an objective view for both him and Zircon, and sets about helping the horse to overcome his fear of wide brightly coloured jumps. They train and practise until Zircon is ready to move forward. The extra work pays dividends when they successfully attempt a similar jump at the next competition.

Mr Rider listens to feedback from across Zircon Ltd. He takes into account the external environment and analyses the factors leading to the failure.

It is obvious that the business had moved forward too soon. Zircon Ltd hadn't been ready; it hadn't been properly prepared. Mr Rider had failed to listen hard enough and had allowed them to be driven by an event, a date on a plan, rather than their level of preparedness. In his haste to achieve he had gone against his own rules and hadn't mitigated all the risks. In fact, he hadn't even seen them; he'd been blind. And his stakeholder engagement? Well, he'd let that go out of the window too.

Having worked through the tough questions that Coach had asked, and putting his pride aside, Mr Rider made the decision to take a sideward step. He would assess, with the business, where their gaps in preparation were and address them. He would look at where the mistakes or errors of judgement had been in order to prevent similar situations in the future. He most certainly wouldn't be apportioning blame as that would achieve nothing, and if it meant repeating or refining some of the work done previously, then so be it. If it meant increased pressure from stakeholders he would handle it. Zircon's future success rested on it. He mentally made a note to reassess the progress made towards the successful achievement of the goal in a month's time.

Then, when Zircon Ltd reattempts the goal after much hard work, the business achieves it and moves forward.

* **TIP:** *Don't be a victim. Pick yourself up, dust yourself down, learn the lessons that need to be learned and move forward.*

The following activities should provide a framework which can go some way to helping you do this:

- View whatever has happened as a blip on your journey, not as an out and out disaster.
- Revisit the plan and the lessons learned previously.
- Revise actions – amending the timeline to realistically reflect activities versus capability.
- Actively engage stakeholders in changes to plans with integrity and honesty, taking care to focus on the individual needs of each stakeholder group.
- Use communication to manage understanding and acceptance of the situation and the proposed solution.

- Be prepared to listen to negative feedback and to handle it in a positive and proactive way.
- Where appropriate, put processes in place to prevent a similar situation occurring again.
- Lead from the front with conviction and rebuild positive momentum, and task your senior team with doing the same.
- Help the organisation regain a positive belief in itself by putting the situation into perspective.

And, above all, continue to believe in yourself and the organisation.

16 LEARN FROM MISTAKES

Although Zircon had overcome his dislike of coloured jumps, Mr Rider knew that it must become a way of being that mistakes were recognised as a matter of course and action taken to prevent them happening again. He decided that he would do an analysis after every competition to learn what had worked well and what hadn't, so that improvements could be made in time for the next competition. To start this process, Mr Rider and the coach undertake an analysis of how Zircon and Mr Rider had fared on completing the cross-country course. They identify strengths and highlight areas which need further work.

If Mr Rider had only listened and made sure that Zircon Ltd was ready to achieve the goal prior to attempting it. If only he'd analysed his risks and mitigated them. If only he hadn't been so driven by his own need to achieve, the company wouldn't have had to experience the setback. The organisation was unsettled and despondent, and he could understand why. People had worked incredibly hard to achieve the goal and it hadn't been down to them that the deadline for its achievement had been unrealistic. Mr Rider acknowledged that his gung-ho attitude had gained them nothing. He had got carried away and believed that things could be achieved by his sheer will alone. Well, they couldn't. This was a partnership.

Mr Rider wouldn't be making the same mistake again. To fail was human, to make the same mistake again would be just plain stupid.

And the business? Well, if it was honest, it could take some responsibility for the setback. Perhaps, just perhaps, it could have communicated its concerns more effectively, perhaps the stronger parts could have supported the weaker parts more, helped them to adopt the new ways of working that would have set them up to achieve the goal. If their leader was big enough to acknowledge his mistakes and learn from them, then so too could the various parts of the business. This was a partnership, after all...

* **TIP:** *We all make mistakes. To learn from them and allow others to learn from them is a strength.*

Mistakes, regardless of whoever makes them (ourselves or others), aren't easy to accept but these pointers should help you.

Reflect – honestly – on what has happened and why things have happened, and encourage the various areas of the organisation to do likewise. Acknowledge where mistakes were made, including your own. Learn to know who you can trust (you really need to listen to these people when they say something won't work) and listen to them on future occasions.

Create a safe environment for your senior team to acknowledge what could work better; this may mean using coaching skills to help your senior managers analyse for themselves what could have ameliorated the problem. Then seek feedback and collective involvement in finding a solution, making sure the feedback loops within your organisation are robust and that your culture supports honest feedback. Talk positively but not insincerely when communicating with the organisation on the situation.

17 DON'T PLAY THE BLAME GAME

Zircon had previously jumped the small ditches without hesitation and Mr Rider imagined that he would be similarly unperturbed about water. However, he resisted instead and then froze. He did not want to move forward; he really, really didn't want to. It didn't feel right. He was all confused and bothered. He just wasn't ready and felt really angry.

Learning from their earlier setback, Mr Rider and Zircon Ltd progress well. They practise, practise and then practise again until new ways of working become habit, only attempting the goals when they are sufficiently prepared to achieve them successfully. They are confident enough to take additional time and a sideward step where necessary, knowing that the extra work involved will pay dividends in the long term and take them nearer the achievement of their overall vision. They handle difficult situations as they arise rather than retreating from them. And, importantly, they keep an eye on the horizon to ensure that the market isn't changing around them and that the business is heading in the direction for which its size and skills are best suited. The business and Mr Rider both realise that they have changed and developed for the better.

But then, once again, they reach an impasse. The business just doesn't seem ready to undertake the next step. Some parts are really dragging their feet. Mr Rider is irritated. He's analysed the situation. He's taken a step sideways, coached, introduced new challenges and, where necessary, repeated work and activities. He believes Zircon has the necessary skills and ability. As he sees it the business is just bucking against the change. Everyone is blaming everyone else: it's back office's fault, they just don't get it and if we fail, it's going to be down to them; sales aren't communicating with us so we don't have a clue about customer demand; accounts aren't invoicing so we're not bringing in cash; we don't understand the new IT systems so aren't processing things quickly...

And it goes on and on, each part of the business blaming another. It wasn't me, it was him/her/them! How many times has Mr Rider heard those words as he has moved up the corporate ladder? How many times has he had them said to him? How many times has he heard them said across Zircon? For that matter, how many times, he's ashamed to admit, has he used them himself? But, he reflects, he has never known blaming to achieve positive results. Why should it? Personally, all he's ever felt when blamed has been negativity and fear, which has ultimately stifled progress. Why should blame achieve a different result across Zircon Ltd?

No, blame wouldn't be something he would be doing. He would lead by example. Blame would be unacceptable right across Zircon.

He looked again at Zircon. He just didn't get what was going wrong.

* TIP: *Don't be tempted to blame.*

Take a clear and unemotional look at what is happening across the business instead of blaming. Consider:

- People;
- Operational;
- IT;
- Customer service;
- Collective working;
- Financial.

Try to understand the behaviours and the reasons for them. Don't get involved in blame apportionment, even during coffee-machine conversations.

Review the culture of the business – where it is now and where it needs to be if the business is to achieve optimum success – and put measures in place to support the journey (i.e. employee performance contracts; sponsorship of the right behaviours, eradication of the wrong ones; personal development plans; open and honest two-way communication). Work with teams within the business to help them learn how to problem solve and manage themselves with confidence, and also work with them to help them understand how to feedback (even negative) information to achieve the most beneficial outcome.

Don't forget to take a forward-looking stance in all communication and stakeholder engagement initiatives; acknowledge the past but don't dwell on it. And when you see blame-oriented behaviours demonstrated you must penalise them.

18 TAKE A BIRD'S EYE VIEW

The coach, in his position as a third party distinct from the horse and rider, has the distinct advantage of being able to take an objective view of the situation. He advises Mr Rider that he needs to ride Zircon forward with confidence and conviction while being careful that he doesn't confuse the horse by giving him mixed

signals and pulling too much on the rein. The coach also feels that Zircon is lacking in confidence and that they should put in place simple training exercises to overcome this.

As a business, Zircon Ltd. feels odd. All the constituent parts of the company know that they have got to change and they 'sort of' know individually what is expected of them. However, knowing is very different to doing.

It feels odd doing things in a different way. The business is in two minds. In reality it feels as if it isn't going anywhere, with the old and new ways of doing things vying for control. If the organisation was honest, the old ways of doing things have now started to feel a bit odd and trying to stick to them is becoming hard work. Working in the new way is getting easier, but that's not to say it still isn't hard work too. Occasionally, when working in the new way, things come together and feel really good, but only occasionally. Zircon begins to feel a bit stuck; nowhere feels easy or nice. The business knows it can't go backwards but forwards is still uncomfortable and, in resisting going forward, it's not going anywhere.

Mr Rider just doesn't seem to be able to pull it together, but he takes stock. He knows where he wants to go. He knows what needs to change in his organisation. He's sure he has communicated it well and engaged stakeholders on all levels. But there's very little forward movement. He listens to feedback across the business. Something's not right but Mr Rider can't put his finger on it. Perhaps he's giving the wrong instructions and support (aids). He just can't tell; he's too close to the problem to view it objectively. He consults Coach.

As an outsider, Coach helps both Mr Rider and Zircon gain some clarity and objectivity around their current situation. Coach is also experienced in helping leaders and businesses understand and manage effective change, and sets about working with both Mr Rider and the business to help each to understand the other's view and work together towards effectively re-establishing forward movement. With hard work and commitment from both sides progress is quickly resumed.

Mr Rider reflects that once again the addition of Coach to the team has accelerated progress and made both him and the people within the organisation think and work in ways that would previously have been deemed impossible. More importantly, these new ways of working and thinking are now learned, internalised and ingrained within the organisation; they won't go when Coach leaves.

It's an interesting one. Mr Rider had always thought that he was at the top of his game. But the way Coach has supported broadening his thinking and the thinking of various parts of the business when they have needed the help has brought out their true potential and heightened their abilities to understand, think more laterally and – ultimately – to achieve.

* **TIP:** *Be open to objective analysis and input.*

This is a hard thing to learn, I know – but try to make the following a matter of habit:

- Standing back and taking an objective view of the organisation.
- Standing back and taking an objective view of the marketplace.
- Encouraging the organisation to take an objective view of itself.
- Encouraging the organisation to collectively seek a solution to its problems.
- Continually reviewing the impact on customers.
- Ensuring the organisation takes steps to address any negative impact on customers.
- Gathering feedback, not just about business but also about the emotional temperature of your organisation.
- Seeking third-party facilitation of views and emotions to encourage clarity and objectivity.
- Remembering that new habits take time and repetition to adopt.
- Bringing in external perspectives: highlight other successful journeys that similar organisations have taken and any opportunities the lessons from these present.

19 WORK AS A PARTNERSHIP – INTERDEPENDENCY

Zircon's movement is balanced, his muscles are working in symmetry; he is no longer simply tolerating Mr Rider but is working in harmony with him with minimal tension. He knows what they need to achieve and what part he, Zircon, needs to play to achieve it. As a result the horse is calm, forward moving and straight. Mr Rider is setting direction, and his instructions and movements are well thought out and clearly and quietly given; he does not try to do Zircon's job for him. Such harmony delivers positive results.

Both Mr Rider and Zircon Ltd progress their partnership. Mr Rider is growing as a leader; he is confident in his leadership, he keeps a constant eye on the horizon for opportunities and threats, he is consistent in how he asks for things – but more importantly he listens and he learns. If he is being told that something is not possible he re-evaluates the situation. He doesn't blame. He looks at what he is being told and how he can remove the barriers to progress. He has noticed that in doing this he is starting to get the best out of each element of the organisation.

The business itself is feeling much better. It's beginning to feel good to be part of Zircon Ltd. It's as though all parts are working together as one seamless whole. It feels more balanced. Yes, it still has its bad days; but that's life. Moving forward feels good, feels natural. In fact, some days Mr Rider doesn't even tell the business what to do. The business just does it, and does it right first time. However, if any part of the organisation requires more support it knows it can have a discussion, and also knows that it will be listened to. Zircon Ltd now feels empowered. It knows that all of its parts can work in harmony. It feels good – different, but good. Very often, Mr Rider just guides. He also praises frequently, and it's good to be praised. The more it's praised, the more the business strives to deliver for Mr Rider. Zircon Ltd flourishes on praise; it's good to be told that you are doing well and to repay the compliment. It's a real partnership now.

Both parties have learned that they can't achieve alone.

* TIP: *You can't do it alone, no matter how charismatic a leader you are – good business is always a team effort!*

Make sure that you empower your people fully…

The leader's role is to set direction and to support the removal of barriers to progress. Ensure that you are not trying to do everything, give your organisation space to grow, allow your organisation to take responsibility for itself. Be very clear in stating where you want

to go, avoiding ambiguity, and don't take knee-jerk actions or display knee-jerk emotions. Listen to and acknowledge feedback; give less-positive feedback when required in a sincere, honest and proactive fashion and, at the same time, always acknowledge good work. Up-skill your people so they are not scared of accepting the challenge, through training and personal development. And acknowledge that you cannot achieve alone, that this is a team effort with all elements of the team being equally responsible for the success of the business.

Remember that the whole is greater than the sum of the parts – believe it!

20 BUCKING FOR ATTENTION

Although Zircon had successfully tackled water jumps with no problem in the past, today he just didn't feel like doing it. He wasn't in the mood. He wanted attention, to be noticed, he wanted his ego stroked, he wanted to test Mr Rider's leadership skills. In short he wanted a reaction – any reaction!

Life is good at Zircon Ltd. The plan is progressing nicely. Many of the goals in it have been achieved; not always on the day shown on the plan, but that doesn't matter – they've been achieved. With the achievement of each goal clearly delivering a benefit, new behaviours and ways of doing things have been learned and become habits.

Mr Rider feels good; the business is pretty much running itself. Its parts are in pretty good shape. It's confident and healthy. They are making good progress towards their vision.

Then the unexpected happens. The mood changes, the business stops moving forward, starts showing old ways and behaviours. Some parts of the business start to underperform and, in short, start to behave badly.

Zircon Ltd is in two minds. It feels odd doing things in a different way. It knows that as a business it has developed well, it knows it's showing real potential; after all, Mr Rider tells it so all the time. But the more it does, the more Mr Rider expects it to do – and for the same amount of reward. Well, it's not going to give in too easily. It knows it can't go backwards, but if it's going to go further forward it wants more attention. It may be immature but that's how it is. It's going to behave badly because it can.

Mr Rider talks the situation through with Coach. They explore the possibilities, look at barriers to moving forward, look at gaps in training or ability. They find none.

* TIP: *Don't panic!*

People are people and we all like attention, some more than others – so don't have knee-jerk reactions. Review the situation instead. Is the behaviour due to a lack of skills or ability, unrealistic timelines or is it more emotional in its nature? Ask yourself whether the behaviour is coming from a particular part of the organisation, and assess whether it is spreading across the organisation as a whole.

Evaluate who the winners and losers of the change initiative are. Are there people the organisation would like to keep but who have, perhaps, suffered as a result of the changes? Maybe these people do require extra positive attention. There may also be people who know they are good and needed, and whose world hasn't changed significantly, but who still feel they should be getting more 'stroking'. As such, they may be misbehaving just because they can and should perhaps not be indulged on this occasion. Base your actions on this evaluation, being careful that you don't unintentionally encourage behaviours you may wish later to eradicate.

21 REWARD ONLY THE RIGHT BEHAVIOUR

Mr Rider, having worked out that there was no underlying reason for Zircon's behaviour, ignored his reaction and didn't rise to the bait. He just kept quietly asking the horse to enter the water ditch. Realising he wasn't getting the reaction he wanted, Zircon eventually sighed and entered the water. Once he had done so, Mr Rider made sure to reward him.

Mr Rider feels winded. What had gone wrong? Zircon Ltd should be agile enough to weather most storms by now, so why had it started to kick up? Why hadn't he seen this coming? Perhaps he was asking his managers to take responsibility for themselves (self-carriage) too far. Maybe he was too hands-off, not strong enough? Or didn't he listen hard enough or hand out praise often enough?

The organisation is getting fed up with receiving so little attention. It knows it is in much better shape than it was before, but it seems that the better it gets the less it gets noticed.

Mr Rider and Coach take a tough decision. They are confident that the business is capable of everything they are asking and has the necessary skills to deliver. They have listened to what it has to say. They are going to do nothing. Mr Rider is going to continue to lead as before. The business needs to grow up, come of age. It has got to work this one out for itself. Mr Rider will not encourage such behaviour.

The business resists and resists and resists, but it is hard work resisting for no return. Mr Rider keeps his nerve, confident that it is a waiting game. He can't allow bad behaviour to be rewarded but keeps the lines of communication open. He doesn't lose patience or focus; he just consistently and calmly asks the business to look and to move forward. With nothing to resist against, Zircon Ltd eventually gets on with the job in hand.

* TIP: *Have the confidence to stick to your guns and reward only the behaviours you wish to encourage.*

Remember, if you are confident that the business has the ability to do what it is being asked to do, just be firm but fair about what is to be achieved. Where people do have a legitimate grievance, be it operational or emotional, address their need in order to remove any barriers to progress. And when the right results are achieved, highlight the success – only this time get the business to highlight it for themselves. Let them take the credit!

22 WHO MOVED THE WINNING POST?

As training progressed, Zircon gained new skills and greater confidence. He had developed both physically and mentally. He was doing well at three-day eventing but Mr Rider had *observed that he had become really first class at show jumping. Through his experiences bringing on Zircon, Mr Rider himself also became more open to looking at new opportunities. He began to realise that, with a slight refocusing of training and exercise, Zircon could become world class at the more commercial and thus more lucrative sport of show jumping.*

Progress is good. The business is in great shape, but then the market shows signs of change. The rules are different. Zircon has also showed signs of excelling in unexpected areas. What to do for the best? Charge on towards the original vision regardless of circumstances, or re-evaluate?

Mr Rider re-evaluates.

Without a doubt the business is now a stronger, more agile, more forward-looking organisation. The key question now is whether the original vision is still the correct one for Zircon Ltd.

Mr Rider, too, has grown in confidence; he has learned much from leading, developing and working with the business. He revisits his original vision. Working with his senior managers, he re-evaluates the benefits and the probability of achieving the vision in the light of the current situation. Together they assess the new opportunities which have opened up for Zircon. Mr Rider takes feedback from across the business and comes to the conclusion that the company in its new improved state can achieve even greater success if it operates in a different arena, if it chooses a slightly different path to that which they had originally selected. He can see that the change in dynamics has potentially opened up a new world of opportunity to the new, improved Zircon. The plan is rescoped to allow them to progress to the achievement of their new vision, making sure to continue maximising the strength of their partnership and thus their chances of success.

* **TIP:** *Don't be afraid to 'wiggle to the left' and adjust your vision to take advantage of market conditions, new opportunities or enhanced capability.*

To have the confidence to make the decision to wiggle you should continually monitor and review:
- Customer feedback;
- Customer needs;
- Financials;
- Progress;
- Skills;
- Strengths;
- The external marketplace (the economy, new competitors, etc.).

Review the original vision as well and check that it is still fit for purpose, given any new/emerging dynamics. Ask yourself whether new potential opportunities have presented themselves which would not have been viable before the change journey was started.

Then, to check your thinking, do scenario planning around new potential opportunities and compare them with the current vision. Road test the strongest scenario with stakeholders, and do a feasibility study of the new scenario.

If everything stacks up, formally adopt a new vision, engaging stakeholders and communicating well. Rescope the original plan, then move forward and monitor progress.

23 THE WINNING POST

And what about Zircon the business and Zircon the horse?

Well, Zircon feels damn good. All the parts are operating well and in unison with one another. It feels much more balanced. Life is much happier and the tension seems to be reduced. Bad days still happen, but somehow new skills seem simpler to acquire, new situations are much less difficult to deal with and new challenges are overcome more easily. It knows it will still encounter difficult situations but is confident that it has the necessary balance to overcome them. Self-carriage is a given and, boy, does that forward movement feel good!

Which Zircon am I talking about now, you ask? The horse or the business? The answer is both – the synergy is complete.

THE END – WHAT END?

It was funny. When writing the story of Zircon the company, I kept on reaching the last chapter and getting stuck. I moaned to a number of my friends and very patient proofreaders that I just couldn't get the ending. And then it dawned on me. There is no ending. That is the whole point.

Change is continuous. Our aim should be to create vibrant, ever-evolving businesses, ones which continually both look and move forward, which have the confidence and the necessary skills, behaviours and agility to handle any conditions which may present themselves.

The harsh fact of life is that if we don't change our business because we feel that it doesn't need changing or are too scared to do so, change will happen around us anyway. It will come and punch us on the nose. It's much better to be in control of our own destiny, to always look forward, to continually improve the way our businesses and us as individuals perform and operate, as a smooth continuum – and as a way of life rather than a knee-jerk reaction.

You have probably bought this book to gain an understanding of how to make change management simple. I hope it has helped you with your quest. Thinking of change simply doesn't make it easy. However, it does make it easier – to understand, to scope, to manage and most importantly to realise those all important benefits. It helps you set yourself up for success.

My personal wish, however, is that change management ceases to exist and that we commit to evolving our businesses, organisations and departments, improving and developing them as 'business as usual', taking away the knee-jerk response. And in the process making them more agile, more able and more confident. Change will then become no big deal but 'the way we do things around here'.

* **HUGE TIP:** *Change is continuous; don't assume anything remains the same. Either we initiate and manage change ourselves and control it or it will happen anyway and control us.*

One last thing...

Interestingly, Victor (the artist) and I, in producing this book, have experienced something of our own change programme. We have, during the course of the process, rescoped our vision, had setbacks, been hit by things outside our control including a major economic downturn – and achieved benefits too numerous to mention. Most importantly, we have developed a really good partnership without which this book could never have been produced. The journey has been fun, frustrating, irritating, rewarding, difficult and most other adjectives (both positive and negative) that you might care to think of.

We have applied the framework throughout. It has got us where we are today; it has kept us on track, helped us to focus, to structure our thoughts and actions, to roll with the punches and last – but not least – to deliver.

One very, very last thing...

Many people have helped me in the writing and publishing of this book. All have given their valuable time willingly (yes, this does mean that I didn't put a knife to their back) to help me in my quest to write this, and their input has been invaluable. But, interestingly, all who have given help and feedback – no matter how senior a business person they were, and luckily for me (or perhaps for you as the reader) I did have some very senior business people helping me – have been very conscious of not offending me or making me feel that they were criticising my work when giving feedback on the book. I have been only too happy to listen and, nine times out of ten, take on board what they had to say. I just wanted to produce a book that I was proud of. I knew that although I like to think of myself as the major star of the whole proceedings (Zircon might fight me for that position), I couldn't do it alone. Although confident in what I knew, I was never naive enough to think that other people couldn't add value. I can safely say that this book is one million times better – OK, I like to exaggerate, but only a little – for their input. And I thank them all very, very much.

On reflection I believe that there is a lesson for us all to learn from my experiences in producing this book. It's often said but not always heeded that when the sums are done correctly (I've added this bit), the sum of the whole is greater than the sum of the parts. From my experience working with changing organisations this is true – and is almost always the difference between quantifiable success or failure in change initiatives.

Forward and onwards...

Since writing this book I have bought a young horse, Dabs. He is a very different kettle of fish to Zircon. Zircon had lots of history, a past that influenced how he thought and moved. Dabs, on the other hand, has very little history.

Zircon very much wanted to walk to his own drumbeat and approached every new way of doing things with caution or complete rejection, and had no desire to be in anyone's gang but his own. Dabs is completely different. He is cautious initially but only because as a youngster he doesn't yet understand how to do many things; however, he loses his caution once he is taught. Prior to starting training, his body didn't really have any coordination, but apart from some elements of his conformation that I just have to accept, he is pretty much a blank canvas and should respond positively to the right training and exercise. To me – and hopefully to you, too, now that I have let you into my world – Zircon very much represents an established company. Dabs, on the other hand... well, he's a start up, isn't he?

I never really had a desire to write a book. I was just so blown away by the synergies of bringing on a horse and bringing on a company that I had to capture the concept and framework. Following this book's completion everyone has asked me if I would write another, to which I replied 'no'. But once again I'm captivated, this time by the link between the young horse and a start-up company that I'm already beginning to see.

So if you are starting a new business, look out for my next book – but be aware it might be a time in coming! I'm a published author now, I walk to my own drumbeat and will go to writing my next book kicking and screaming no matter who leads me. All right, I'm very well behaved really so I possibly won't scream – but I think you get the picture!

INDEX

Index compiled by Meg Davies
(Fellow of the Society of Indexers)